The Story of a Special Day
Volume 276

October

2

*The 275th day of the year (276th in leap years).
There are 90 days remaining until the end of the year.*

by Michael Dobson

Timespinner
Press

Watch for e-book editions for Kindle, e-pub devices, and other formats from your favorite online booksellers.

For more information about the series, about us, or about your special day, please email us at editor@timespinnerpress.com.

Look for other volumes in *The Story of a Special Day,* coming often. See www.timespinnerpress.com for details and for the most recent information.

Table of Contents

For the definition of "O.S.," "CE," and "BCE" used with some dates , see the section "On Names and Dates."

Cover: Mohandas (Mahatma) Gandhi, Indian independence leader, born October 2, 1869 — see the COVER STORY/PERSON OF THE DAY

Quote of the Day

"My centre is giving way, my right is retreating, situation excellent, I am attacking." *(Mon centre cède, ma droite recule, situation excellente, j'attaque.)*

Ferdinand Foch, French general,
Allied Supreme Commander, World War I
born October 2, 1851.

Today
in
History
October 2

US President Woodrow Wilson — Wilson suffered a stroke on October 2, 1919, leaving him partially paralyzed.

October 2 in History

While some days of the year are more famous than others, every day of the year is filled with important, exciting, and unusual events, from religious awakenings to natural disasters, from wars to breakthroughs in technology, and from tragedy to triumph.

In this section, you'll learn about all the events that make October 2 important, including the special event that makes up our cover story or event of the day. Some events you may already know about, others may be new to you, but all of them are important parts of the history of the work.

Let's explore some of the reasons why October 2 is a very special day!

                                              Michael Dobson

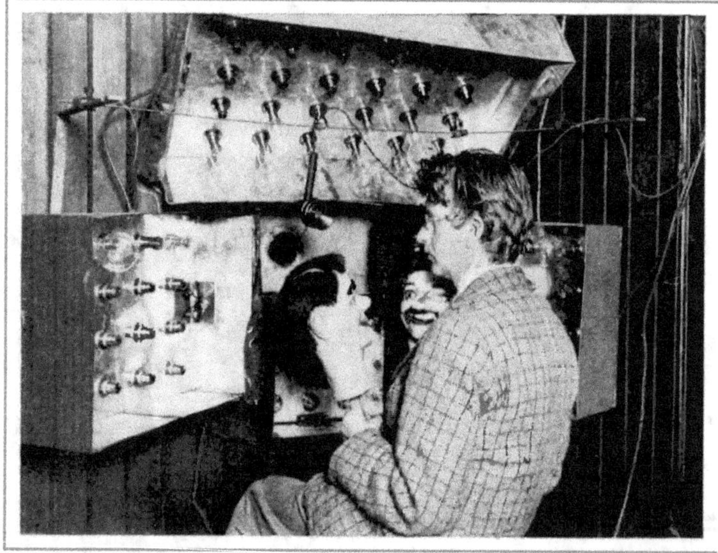

John Logie Baird and the first publicly demonstrated television system, featuring ventriloquist dummies "James" and "Stooky Bill." Baird transmitted the first television image on October 2, 1925 — the EVENT OF THE DAY

What Happened on October 2?

From the creation of great works of engineering and art, to devastating wars and natural disasters, thousands of years of history have left their mark on each and every day of the year. Here are some important events that occurred on October 2. (Items with a photo or illustration are boxed.)

1187 — **Saladin conquers the city of Jerusalem**; Europe launches the Third Crusade in response.

1535 — French explorer **Jacques Cartier** first reaches what later becomes the city of **Montreal.**

1835 — The **Texas Revolution begins** as a hastily assembled militia resists Mexican soldiers at the Battle of Gonzales.

1919 — US President **Woodrow Wilson suffers a stroke** that leaves him partially paralyzed and blind; his wife and other advisors keep his condition private, unwilling to admit he was unable to perform his duties as President. *(Photo page 4.)*

John Logie Baird — successfully transmitted the first television picture on October 2, 1925

Event of the Day
1925 - First Television Transmission

A number of inventors and engineers contributed to the development of television, including Alexander Bain (inventor of the fax), Paul Nipkow, Constantin Perskyi (who coined the word "television"), Lee de Forest, Arthur Korn, and others.

The first person to. build and test a working television set, however, was Scottish engineer John Logie Baird. His prototype was made from an old hatbox, with darning needles, bicycle light lenses, and a used tea set. On October 2, 1925, Baird successfully transmitted the first television picture. It consisted of the head of a ventriloquist's dummy (named "Snooky Bill"), with 30 scan lines at five pictures per section. (By contrast, an HD television image has 1080 scan lines at 50 to 60 pictures per second.)

When Baird took his story to the local newspaper to promote his invention, the news editor said, "For God's sake, go down to reception and get rid of a lunatic who's down there. He says he's got a machine for seeing by wireless! Watch him — he may have a razor on him."

In spite of this setback,Baird demonstrated his invention publicly in January 1926. He is named one of the 10 greatest Scottish scientists in history and was number 44 on BBC's list of the "100 Greatest Britons."

1928 — The Prelature of the Holy Cross and **Opus Dei**, a personal prelature of the Roman Catholic Church, is founded. Today, the organization has nearly 100,000 members worldwide.

Opus Dei cross

1937 — Dominican leader Rafael Trujillo orders the **Parsley Massacre** (*el corte* or *kout kouto-a*) of Hatian Creoles; estimates of the number killed range from 1,000 to over 12,000.

1941 — The **Battle of Moscow** begins with the launch of the German offensive Operation Typhoon The campaign lasts until January 7, 1942, with a decisive Soviet victory and the beginning of the overall German defeat.

1950 — The comic strip *Peanuts,* by Charles M. Schultz, premiers.

First published *Peanuts* comic, October 2, 1950 (© 2005 United Features Syndicate)

1959 — The television series *The Twilight Zone* **premiers** on CBS.

The Twilight Zone logo from the opening credits

1970 — An airplane carrying members of the **Wichita State Univesity football team crashes,** killing 31 people.

1980 — Pennsylvania Congressman Michael Myers becomes the **first member of the US House of Representatives to be expelled since 1861** after his involvement in the Abscam scandal.

2002 — The **Beltway sniper attacks** begin. Ten people are killed and three critically wounded before the killers, John Allen Muhammad and Lee Boyd Malvo, are captured.

2006 — **Eight Amish school girls are shot** and five killed in the West Nickel Mines School shooting. The Amish community's emphasis on forgiveness and reconciliation received national attention.

Labors of the Months: October, by Simon Bening

Quote of the Day

"The weak can never forgive. Forgiveness is the attribute of the strong."

Mohandas K. Gandhi, revolutionary leader
born October 2, 1869

Births
and
Deaths

October 2

                                    Michael Dobson

Mahatma Gandhi, Indian independence leader, born October 2, 1869 — the COVER STORY and PERSON OF THE DAY

Notable October 2 People

With the current world population at about seven billion people, on average about 19 million people also celebrate their birthdays on October 2 — and that isn't counting millions and millions who came before! No matter when you were born, you share your birthday with many special people whose accomplishments (and occasionally embarrassments) have been noted as part of history.

In this section, you'll meet fascinating people who share your birthday, or who died on this day in history. They're organized by what they're famous for, and then in reverse chronological order from most recent to earliest. Those who are shown in photographs or artwork have a box around them. We don't have photos of everyone, so please forgive us if your favorite person is missing.

Some of these people you've heard of, others will be new to you, but they all make up an important part of the reason that October 2 is a truly special day!

Groucho Marx, born October 2, 1890

Who Was Born on October 2?

Art and Photography

Annie Liebovitz, American portrait photographer, first woman to have an exhibition at Washington's National Portrait Gallery. *(1949)*

Alex Raymond, American cartoonist best known as the creator of Flash Gordon. *(1909)*

The March 4, 1934. newspaper strip of *Flash Gordon* by Alex Raymond (© 1934, 1990 King Features Syndicate)

Fashion

Donna Karan, American fashion designer who created the DKNY brand. *(1948)*

Government and Politics

Cordell Hull, longest-serving US Secretary of State, served under President Franklin D. Roosevelt for the majority of World War II. Received the 1945 Nobel Peace Prize for his role in establishing the United Nations. *(1871)*

Mohandas K. Gandhi as an attorney in South Africa, 1909

Cover Story/Person of the Day
Mahatma Gandhi (1869)

Mohandas Karamchand Gandhi played a pivotal role as leader of the Indian independence movement from British control. He created the powerful philosophy known as *satyagraya,* a non-violent form of civil disobedience that uses "soul force" as a political means, a major influence on such figures as Martin Luther King, Jr., and Nelson Mandela. He is often referred to as *Mahatma,* a Sanskrit honorific meaning "high-souled" or "venerable."

Gandhi was born October 2, 1869, in Gujarat, a western Indian state. Trained as a lawyer, he worked in South Africa, supporting the Indian community's struggle for civil rights.

In 1915, he returned to India, where he began organizing peasants, farmers, and urban laborers to protest against excessive taxation and discrimination, and in 1921 became head of the Indian National Congress in its campaign for Indian self-rule.

One of his most famous protests is known as the Salt March, a 24-day march protesting British taxation that made it illegal for Indians to reclaim sea salt from the ocean. He was arrested, and it took more than a year of protests to eliminate the tax, but it galvanized national resistance to British rule.

He fought for a united India practicing religious pluralism, but ultimately the subcontinent was partitioned into Hindu India and Muslim Pakistan. His attempt to make peace between the parties led to his assassination in 1948 by a Hindu nationalist.

Paul von Hindenburg, German military and political leader. As President of Germany, he appointed Hitler as Chancellor of that nation. *(1847)*

Richard III of England, last king of the House of York and last of the Plantagenet dynasty, subject of Shakespeare's play *Richard III*. His defeat and death at the Battle of Bosworth Field was the last decisive battle of the Wars of the Roses and marked the end of the Middle Ages in England. *(1452)*

Earliest known portrait of Richard III, painted circa 1520

Law

Johnnie Cochran, American attorney best known for his defense of O. J. Simpson in the murder of his former wife; also defended such high-profile clients as Michael Jackson, Tupac Shakur, Jim Brown, Snoop Dogg, and others. *(1937)*

Letters

Vernor Vinge, American science fiction author who received the Hugo Award for various novels and novellas, including *A Fire Upon the Deep* and *Rainbow's End. (1944)*

Rex Reed, American film critic for the New York *Observer* and former co-host of the television show *At the Movies. (1938)*

Jack Finney, American author best known for his novels *The Body Snatchers* (made into a film several times) and *Time and Again. (1911)*

Graham Greene, prolific novelist regarded as one of the great writers of the 20th century, famous for such works as *The Quiet American, Our Man in Havana,* and the screenplay for the film *The Third Man. (1904)*

Wallace Stevens, American modernist poet who won the Pulitzer Prize for Poetry and the National Book Award for Poetry (twice). *(1879)*

Music

Tiffany, singer-songwriter and teen icon whose eponymous debut album and single hit No. 1 on the *Billboard* Hot 100 chart. *(1955)*

Philip Oakey, singer-songwriter best known as co-founder of the synthpop band The Human League. *(1955)*

Sting, English musician known as the principal songwriter, lead singer, and bassist for the new wave band The Police before embarking on a successful solo career.. *(1951)*

Sting in 2007 (Photo: Lionel Urman, CC BY-SA 3.0)

Chris LeDoux, country music singer-songwriter who recorded 36 albums, also was a Hall of Fame rodeo champion. *(1948)*

Don McLean, American singer-songwriter best known for his 1971 hit "American Pie," voted No. 5 in the RIAA list of Songs of the Century. *(1945)*

Performing Arts

Paul Teutul, Jr., motorcycle designer and fabricator who co-founded Orange County Choppers, featured in the reality television series *American Chopper.* *(1974)*

Kelly Ripa, actress known for her portrayal of Hayley on the daytime drama *All My Children*, and as co-host of the syndicated talk show *Live! with Kelly and Ryan*; named one of the most powerful people in media in 2014 by *The Hollywood Reporter.* *(1970)*

Lorraine Bracco, actress nominated for the Best Supporting Actress Oscar for her role in *Goodfellas,* also known for her roles in the TV series *The Sopranos* and *Rizzoli & Isles.* *(1954)*

Persis Khambatta, Indian model and actress named Femina Miss India in 1965, best known to American audiences for her role in the 1979 film *Star Trek: The Motion Picture.* *(1948)*

                                          Michael Dobson

Bud Abbott (left) with Lou Costello

Moses Gunn, actor who founded the Negro Ensemble Company, received two Obie Awards for his stage roles. *(1929)*

George "Spanky" McFarland, child star best known for his role in the *Our Gang/Little Rascals* short films. *(1928)*

George McFarland as "Spanky"

Bud Abbott, comedian known as the straight man of the comedy duo Abbott and Costello. *(1897)*

Groucho Marx, comedian, film and television star, and writer, known for his films with his siblings the Marx Brothers and as host of the TV game show *You Bet Your Life*. *(1890)* *(Photo page 18.)*

Science and Medicine

John Gurdon, English biologist who shared the 2012 Nobel Prize for Physiology or Medicine for the discovery that mature cells could be converted to stem cells. *(1933)*

Christian de Duve, Belgian cytologist and biochemist who shared the 1974 Nobel Prize in Physiology or Medicine for discoveries concerning the structural and functional organizaiton of the cell. *(1917)*

Alexander R. Todd, British biochemist who received the 1957 Nobel Prize for Chemistry for his work on nucleotides. *(1907)*

William Ramsay, British chemist who received the 1904 Nobel Prize in Chemistry for discovering the inert gaseous elements in air. *(1852)*

Sports

Jana Novotná, Czech tennis player ranked World No. 2 tennis player in 1997, won 12 Grand Slam women's doubles titles. *(1968)*

Thomas Muster, Austrian tennis player ranked World No. 1 tennis player in 1996; won eight Masters 1000 series titles. *(1967)*

Mark Rypien, first Canadian NFL quarterback to win the Superbowl MVP Award. *(1962)*

Glenn Anderson, played 16 seasons in the NHL, primarily for the Edmonton Oilers; inducted into the Hockey Hall of Fame in 2008. *(1960)*

John Cook, golfer ranked in the top ten of the Official World Golf Ratings for 45 weeks in the early 1990s, won eleven times on the PGA Tour. *(1957)*

Dick Barnett, basketball player known for his nine seasons with the New York Knicks. *(1936)*

Earl Wilson, baseball player and coach who played as a starting pitcher for the Boston Red Sox, the Detroit Tigers, and the San Diego Padres. *(1934)*

Maury Wills, baseball player and manager who played for the Los Angeles Dodgers, the Pittsburgh Pirates, and the Montreal Expos; credited for reviving the stolen base as part of baseball strategy. *(1932)*

Sir Pelham "Plum" Warner, Test cricketer known as "the Grand Old Man" of English cricket, knighted in 1937 for his contributions to the game. *(1873)*

War and Revolution

Ferdinand Foch, French military leader and theorist who served as Supreme Allied Commander during World War I, creating the final Allied strategy that won the land war in western Europe. *(1851)*

Nat Turner, enslaved African-American who led a slave rebellion in Virginia in 1831. Over 200 blacks and more than 50 whites were killed or executed, including Turner. *(1800)*

"Discovery of Nat Turner," by William Henry Shelton

Ferdinand Foch (Photo: Melcy)

"Nude Descending a Staircase No. 2," by Marcel Duchamp (1912)
(Collection of the Philadelphia Museum of Art)

Who Died on October 2?

Art and Illustration

Marcel Duchamp, painter, sculptor, and writer credited (along with Picasso and Matisse) as helping to define the arts during the revolutionary first decades of the 20th century. *(1968)*

Sarah Biffin, Victorian English painter born without arms and with only vestigial legs. She learned to write with her mouth, as well as do needlework and use scissors. She became a skilled painter of landscapes and portrait miniatures, for which she received a medal from the Society of Artists of Great Britain and acceptance of her paintings by the Royal Academy of Arts. *(1850)*

Self-portrait by Sarah Biffin

Government and Military

Samuel Adams, one of the Founding Fathers of the United States, revolutionary leader, philosopher, and statesman; namesake of Samuel Adams beer. *(1803)*

John André, British Army officer hanged by the Continental Army as a spy for assisting Benedict Arnold's attempted surrender of West Point to the British. *(1780)*

Self-portrait by Major John André, drawn on the eve of his execution.

Literature and Poetry

August Wilson, American playwright whose 10-play opus *The Pittsburgh Cycle* received two Pulitzer Prizes. *(2005)*

Harry Golden, Jewish-American writer and newspaper publisher, known for such books as *For 2¢ Plain* and *Only in America.* *(1981)*

Fukuda Chiyo-ni (Kaga no Chiyo) (福田千代尼), Japanese Edo era Buddhist nun and poet regarded as one of the greatest female haiku poets.. *(1775)*

"Fukuda Chiyo-ni" by Utagawa Kuniyoshi, illustrating her haiku:

"Morning glory
the well bucket-entangled
I ask for water."

Performing Arts

Nipsey Russell, American comedian best remembered for his numerous game show appearances. *(2005)*

Gene Autry, singing cowboy and Western star in the movies, TV, and radio. Also wrote hit songs including "Back in the Saddle Again," "Frosty the Snowman," and "Rudolph the Red-Nosed Reindeer." *(1998)*

Gene Autry

Harriet Nelson, singer and actress best known for her role on the classic sitcom *The Adventures of Ozzie and Harriet.(1987)*

Harriet (left) and Ozzie Nelson

Madeleine Carroll, English actress once the highest-paid actress in the world, best remembered for her role in Hitchcock's *The 39 Steps. (1987)*

Rock Hudson, popular leading man during the Hollywood Golden Age, known for numerous comedies with Doris Day as well as adventure films including *Tobruk* and *Ice Station Zebra. (1985)*

Rock Hudson

Hazel Scott, actress, pianist, and singer, host of *The Hazel Scott Show* (1950), the first television show hosted by a person of color. *(1981)*

Hazel Scott in *Rhapsody in Blue* (1945)

Religion and Mysticism

P. D. Ouspensky, Russian mathematician and mystic known for his work with the doctrines of George Gurdjieff, chronicled in his book *In Search of the Miraculous. (1947)*

Science and Technology

> **Sir Alec Issigonis,** British-Greek car designer known for creating the Mini. *(1988)*

Sir Alec Issigonis standing between the original Mini (621 AOK, left), and a new 1965 Morris Mini Minor Deluxe
(British Museums Trust, CC BY-SA 4.0)

Sir Peter Medawar, Brazilian-born British biologist who shared the 1960 Nobel Prize in Physiology or Medicine for the discovery of acquired immunological tolerance. *(1987)*

Svante Arrhenius, received the 1903 Nobel Prize in Chemistry for using physical chemistry to calculate the relationship between atmospheric carbon dioxide and surface temperature of the Earth, the basis of determining that human-caused CO_2 emissions are causing climate change. *(1927)*

Nicholas-Joseph Cugnot, French inventor credited with building the first working self-propelled land-based mechanical vehicle — the world's first automobile. *(1804)*

Nicholas Cugnot's "Fardier à vapeur", the first self moving vehicle.in what is possibly the world's first automobile accident

Quote of the Day

"A petty reason perhaps why novelists more and more try to keep a distance from journalists is that novelists are trying to write the truth and journalists are trying to write fiction."

Graham Greene, novelist
born October 2, 1904

Holidays Around the World

October 2

Painting of Raden Aria Kusuma di Niggrat, Regent of Galuh, wearing traditional Indonesian batik — for BATIK DAY

Holidays Around the World

If you're looking for a reason to take your special day off, you should know that every single day is a holiday somewhere in the world! Here's some of what you can celebrate on October 2!

October 2 General Events

Batik Day (Indonesia)

Batik, the traditional cloth of Indonesia, is celebrated on October 2, the date it was officially recognized by UNESCO as a "Masterpiece of Oral and Intangible Heritage of Humanity." Celebrate by wearing batik on this day.

Gandhi Jayanti (India)

Gandhi's birthday is celebrated with a national festival in India, where it is one of the three national holidays of the country.

Independence Day (Republic of Guinea)

The West African nation of Guinea celebrates its independence from France, declared October 2, 1958.

International Day of Non-Violence (UN member states)

Gandhi's birthday is also designated by the UN General Assembly as the International Day of Non-Violence.

National Grandparents' Day (Italy)

Italy's *Festa Nazionale dei Nonni* is celebrated on October 2, the Memorial of the Holy Guardian Angels feast in the Roman Catholic Church. (*See Religious Feast Days and Holidays.*)

World Day for Farmed Animals (various organizations)

The Farm Animal Rights Movement uses Gandhi's birthday as the occasion World Day for Farmed Animals, a protest against abuses in animal farming.

October 2 Food Holidays

National Fried Scallops Day (US)

In the United States, almost every day of the year is dedicated to a particular food. (Some other countries do this also, but not every day.) Sponsored by manufacturers, retailers, farmers, or simply fans, these days are often proclaimed by the President, Congress, state governors, or mayors. Given that there are more different foods than days of the year, some days honor more than one kind of food! So for dinner, how about some tasty fried scallops?

Honorary Food Months

In addition, the entire month of October is used to celebrate numerous foods. Here's a list of what to eat in the month of October!

(Photo: Christo, CC BY-SA 4.0)

- National Apple Month
- National Applejack Month
- National Caramel Month
- National Cookie Month
- National Dessert Month
- National Pasta Month
- National Pickled Peppers Month
- National Pizza Month
- National Popcorn Poppin' Month
- National Pork Month
- National Pretzel Month
- National Seafood Month

Ángel de la Guarda, for MEMORIAL OF THE HOLY GUARDIAN
ANGELS

Religious Feast Days and Holidays

Mehregan (مهرگان) (Zoroastrian and Persian communities)

The Zorastrian deity Mithra (Mehr in Persian) is honored on the 196th day of the year according to the Zoroastrian calendar, which has March 21 (Nowruz) as its new year's day, so depending on the year it is celebrated either October 1 or October 2. While it was a major festival in the ancient Persian festival, now it is celebrated with a religious ceremony around a colorful table during lunchtime.

Memorial of the Holy Guardian Angels (Roman Catholicism)

This Catholic feast has been celebrated in one form or another since the 4th century.

Saint Days

Each day in the year is considered a feast day for one or more saints. October 2 is the feast day of Saints Leodegarius, Damaris of Athens, Beregisus, Ursicinus, and Cassian the Greek.

Moveable and Multi-Day Events

Some events take place over a specific week or time period. Start and finish dates may vary from year to year. Some events occur on different days each year (such as "fourth Saturday of a month"). These events sometimes include or take place on October 2.

Week-Long Celebrations

- Customer Service Week (US and Kenya)
- Mental Illness Awareness Week (US)

Movable Events

First Sunday

- Day of Prayer for the Peace of Jerusalem (Pentecostal)
- Father's Day (Luxembourg)
- Teacher's Day (Belarus and Latvia)

First Monday

- Child Health Day (US)
- Children's Day (Chile and Singapore)
- Territory Day (Christmas Island)
- Thanksgiving (Saint Lucia)
- World Architecture Day
- World Habitat Day

October Honorary Months

Presidents, Congresses, and nations around the world issue proclamations recognizing particular months to honor certain causes. These events generally fall in October, though honorary months do come and go. Holidays established by states and nonprofit organizations are listed if verified.

If not otherwise specified, all months are US. There is some variation from year to year; some celebratory months get added and others get dropped. Two places to get up to date information are the current edition of *Chase's Calendar of Events* or the website Brownielocks.

Here are some honorary designations for October.

Culture

- Black History Month (UK)
- Filipino American History Month
- German American Heritage Month (September 15-October 15 in the US)
- Hispanic Heritage Month (September 15-October 15 in the US)
- Italian American Heritage Month
- LGBT History Month
- Polish American Heritage Month

Health

- American Pharmacists Month
- Brain Tumor Awareness Month (Canada)
- Breast Cancer Awareness Month
- Dental Hygiene Month
- Down Syndrome Awareness Month
- Dwarfism/Little People Awareness Month
- Dyslexia Awareness Month
- Eczema Awareness Month
- Health Literacy Month
- Healthy Lung Month
- Infertility Awareness Month
- Liver Awareness Month
- Medical Ultrasound Awareness Month
- Physical Therapy Month
- Spina Bifida Awareness Month
- Sudden Infant Death Syndrome (SIDS) Awareness Month
- World Blindness Awareness Month

Other

- Bat Appreciation Month
- Black Speculative Fiction Month
- Caffeine Addiction Recovery Month
- Church Library Month
- Class Reunion Month
- Domestic Violence Awareness Month
- Fair Trade Month
- Feral Hog Month
- Financial Planning Month

- International Walk to School Month
- National Adopt a Shelter Dog Month
- National Arts and Humanities Month

Just for Fun

Anybody can make up a holiday, and many people do! While none of these are officially recognized and some may come and go, here are a few more holidays for October 2.

- *Peanuts* Day (celebrating the cartoon)

- Phileas Fogg's Wager Day (from Jules Verne's *Around the World in Eighty Days*)

Phileas Fogg's Bet, by Alphone de Neuville and Léon Benett, illustrating Jules Verne's *Around the World in Eighty Days* (1872)

Quote of the Day

"I'm so glad I live in a world where there are Octobers. "

Lucy Maud Montgomery
in *Anne of Green Gables*

About
the
Month
of

THER
ACC
MAGNA

October

"October" from the *Brevarium Grimani* by Simon Bening (c.1510)

October: The Tenth Month

The sweet calm sunshine of October, now
Warms the low spot; upon its grassy mould
The purple oak-leaf falls; the birchen bough
Drops its bright spoil like arrow-heads of gold.

— "October," William Cullen Bryant

In Latin, *octo* means eight, so it may seem odd that October is actually the tenth month! The reason goes back to the early Roman calendar, which began the new year in March. What about January and February? They didn't exist, because winter was considered a "monthless" period. Those two months didn't join the calendar until 713 BCE, pushing October from eighth to tenth in the calendar year.

Whether it's the eighth or the tenth month, October has always had 31 days. The last day of October and the last day of February end on the same day of the week in both regular and leap years.

From a seasonal point of view, October is the second month of autumn in the Northern Hemisphere and the second month of spring Down Under. October is the equivalent of April in the other hemisphere.

As an odd bit of trivia, more US presidents have been born in October than any other month: John Adams, Rutherford B. Hayes, Chester A. Arthur, Theodore Roosevelt, and Jimmy Carter.

October in Other Cultures

The month of October has different names in different languages. Some are very similar to English (octobre, oktober, etc.), while some are quite different. Some nations use calendars other than the Gregorian, and their months may overlap with October. In lunar-based calendars, such as the Islamic calendar, months move through the seasons, but many of these languages have a word for October.

Albanian: Tetor

Anglo-Saxon: Wyn-monath (wine month)

Arabic (Egypt, Sudan, Yemen): يونأغينافبرايتشرين الأَكتوبر (uktūbar)

Arabic (Levant): حزيركانوشباتشرين الأول (tishrīn al-awwal)

Arabic (Libya): الصهناالنالتمور، الثمور (at-tumūr; al-tumūr)

Arabic (Morocco, Algeria, and Tunisia): جأَيفيفرأكتوبر، أوكتوبر (uktūbər; ūktūbər)

Azerbaijani: Oktyabrl

Basque: Urri

Chinese: 十月 (Cantonese: sahpyuht; Mandarin: shíyuè; Taiwanese: chap-goeh)

Croatian: Listopad

Czech: říjen

Finnish: Lokakuu

Greek: Οκτώβριος (Októbrios)

Haitian Creole: Oktòb

Hebrew: ינפברואוקטובר (ôqtôber)

Hindi: अक्टूबर (aktūbar)

Irish (Gaelic): Deireadh Fómhair mí Dheireadh Fómhair

Italian: Ottobre

Japanese (traditional calendar): 十月 (jūgatsu); 神無月 (kaminaduki)

Khoekhoe (Nama): ǂnûǀǀnâiseb

Korean: 시월 (siweol)

Lithuanian: Spalis

Manx: Jerrey-fouyir

Maori: Whiringa ā nuku

Old English: Winterfylleþ

Polish: Październik

Quechua: Kantarayki

Russian: октябрь (oktjabr')

Sardinian: Ladàmini

Scottish Gaelic: an t-Sultain

Sesotho: Mphalane

Spanish: Febrero

Swahili: Oktoba

Swazi: iMphala

Thai: Tulakhom

Turkish: Ekim

Ukrainian: жовтень (zhovten)

Vietnamese: 腩迣 (tháng mười)

Welsh: Hydref

Yiddish: פעברואַאָקטאָבבער (oktober)

Zulu: uOkthoba

October Sayings and Superstitions

Here are some sayings and superstitions associated with the month of October.

October Weather Superstitions

Rain in October means wind in December.

When birds and badgers are fat in October, expect a cold winter.

When berries are many in October, beware a hard winter.

If ducks do slide at Hallowtide, at Christmas they will swim; if ducks do swim at Hallowtide, at Christmas they will slide.

There will always be 29 fine days in October.

If the October moon comes without frost, expect no frost till the moon of November.

Halloween Superstitions

If you see bats flying around your house on Halloween, ghosts and spirits are nearby.

If you go to a crossroads at Halloween and listen to the wind, you will learn all the most important things that will befall you during the next twelve months.

Children born on Halloween are said to have the gift of second sight, and can ward off evil spirits.

If you see a spider on Halloween night, it means the spirit of a departed loved one is watching over you.

If you ring bells on Halloween, you will chase away evil spirits.

And if you want to meet a witch, put your clothes on inside out and walk backwards on Halloween night!

October Wedding Superstitions

If in October you do marry, love will come but riches tarry.

The three luckiest months for a wedding are June, October, and December.

An October bride will be pretty, coquettish, loving, but jealous.

Married when leaves in October thin, toil and hardships for you begin.

October Symbols

Birthstones by Culture: Although a variety of birthstones have been associated with each month, the National Association of Jewelers adopted an official list of stones for each birth month. For October, the stones are *opal* and *tourmaline*.

Other stones associated with October include *aquamarine* and *coral*. There are also birthstones associated with the signs of the zodiac. For October, Libra (9/23-10/23) is associated with *chrysolite*, and Scorpio (10/24-11/21) with *beryl*.[*]

Birth Flowers: *Calendula,* also known as *Marigold,* or *Cosmos.* It is associated with warmth, elegance, and devotion, as well as comfort and healing.

Birth Tree: The ancient Druids associated trees with different months of the year. For people born between September 30 and October 27, the birth tree is *ivy.* From October 28 through November 24, it is the *reed.*

---

[*] In sidereal astronomy (see "October 2 Zodiac Signs" for specifics), people born between October 1 and October 17 are considered Virgos. Virgo's birthstone is *carnelian.*

"October," by Eugène Grasset

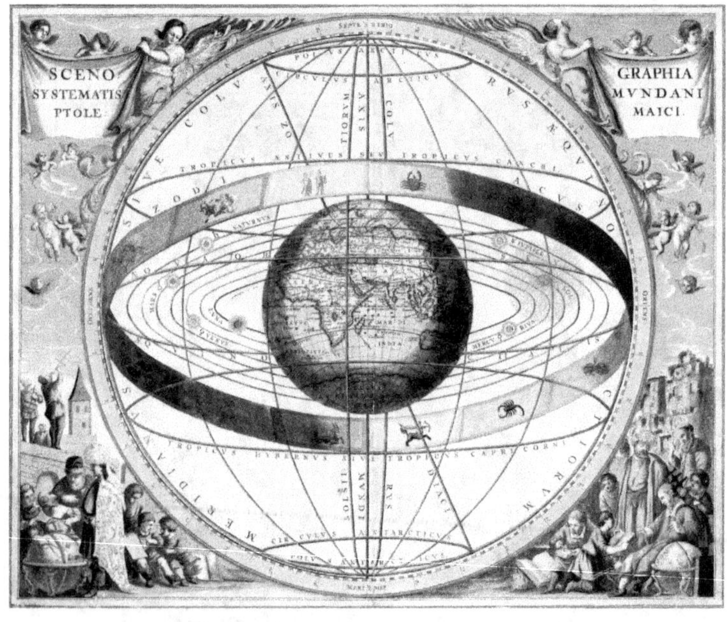

Scenography of the Ptolemaic Cosmography, by Johannes van Loon, based on Andreas Cellarius's *Harmonia Macrocosmica,* 1660

October 2 Zodiac Signs

From the perspective of someone on Earth, the Sun appears to move through the sky throughout the year, along a path astronomers call the *ecliptic plane*. The ecliptic plane is divided into twelve constellations, known as the zodiac, based on traditionally observed patterns of stars. On your birthday, you can't see your constellation, because it's in the daytime sky.

The zodiac was first developed by Babylonian astronomers about 2,500 years ago. Because they were unaware that the Earth wobbles like a spinning top (known as *precession*), they didn't make allowance for the fact that the Sun's path through the zodiac changes over time.

That means there are now two sets of dates for your birth sign. The *tropical dates* are the original Babylonian dates; the *sidereal dates* tell you where the Sun actually appears as it moves along its annual path.

For October 2, the tropical sign is **Libra** and the sidereal sign is **Virgo.**

Libra

Tropical September 23 to October 23
Sidereal October 16 to November 15

The Babylonians considered Libra, the Scales, to be sacred to the sun god Shamash, patron of truth and justice. The Romans reassigned the scales to Astraea, the celestial virgin, better known as Virgo.

Libra is symbolized by the gryphon, a mythological creature with the head, wings, and claws of an eagle and the hind legs of a lion. The Romans believed Libra was the sign "in which the seasons are balanced," and thus idolized this constellation.

Libra is an air sign, and people born under this sign are supposed to be extroverts, socially graceful, and just. Librans are supposed to be compatible with the other air signs of Gemini and Aquarius.

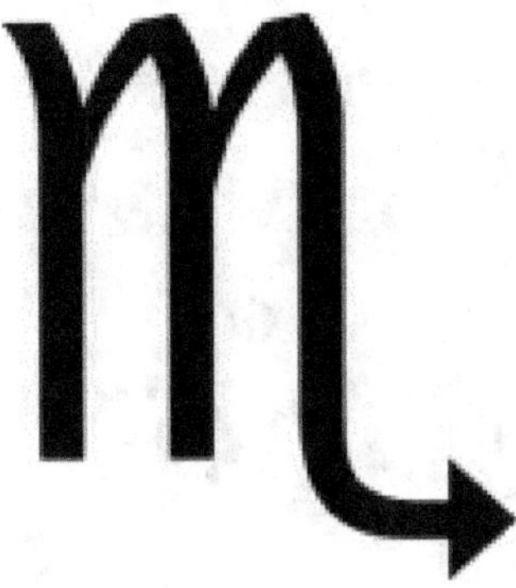

Virgo

Tropical August 23 to September 22
Sidereal September 16 to October 15

The constellation Virgo is the second-largest constellation in the night sky. Its brightest star, Spica, makes it easy to locate. If you can find the Big Dipper (Ursa Major), follow the curve in the Dipper's handle. The second bright star you see is Spica.

In Greek and Roman mythology, Virgo is associated with Demeter (Ceres), the goddess of wheat, and also with Erigone and Astraea. In astrology, Virgo is known as a "mutable sign." It's associated with being reflective and receptive to the ideas of others, sensitive to criticism, and oriented toward detail and precision.

Virgos are supposed to be compatible with Capricorn, Taurus, Cancer, and Scorpio, and to a lesser extent with Virgo and Pisces.

Illustration by Edward Penfield

What Day of the Week is October 2?

On what day of the week does October 2 fall?

Surprisingly, this isn't an easy question. Because the calendar year is 365 days long (366 in leap years), it doesn't divide evenly by the seven days of the week.

Also, the Earth goes around the Sun in about 365-1/4 days, so a calendar tends to drift over time. That's why the same date falls on different weekdays in different years.

This is made even more complicated by a change in calendars that took place in 1582. Our modern calendar has its roots in ancient Rome, in a calendar reform conducted by Julius Caesar. Caesar commissioned mathematicians to attack the problem, and they came up with the idea of leap years, and thus standardized the calendar for centuries to come. This was called the Julian calendar.

Over time, however, the small errors in Caesar's calculation compounded. That's why Pope Gregory XIII commissioned the Gregorian calendar, used in most of the world today. Some countries converted in 1582, when the calendar was first developed; some converted later; other still haven't changed.

Gregorian and Julian aren't the only types of calendars. The Hebrew year, the Islamic year, and many other calendars are used in different parts of the world and among different people.

You can convert Gregorian dates to other calendars, including the Hebrew calendar, the Islamic calendar, and even the Mayan calendar by visiting the Fourmilab Calendar Converter at http://www.fourmilab.ch/documents/calendar/.

Chinese calendar systems are quite complex and have changed several times; a full discussion is far beyond the scope of this book. If you're interested, you can find information here: http://www.hermetic.ch/cal_stud/chinese_cal.htm.

On Names and Dates

Historians use "CE" (Common Era) and "BCE" (Before the Common Era) instead of the more common "AD" (Anno Domini, or Year of Our Lord) and "BC" (Before Christ), reflecting the fact that the year-numbering system established by the Gregorian calendar is used throughout the world in many countries not culturally Christian.

The CE/BCE designation dates back to at least 1708, and has been adopted as a standard by the United Nations and the Universal Postal Union. Because this series of books covers events and people of all nations and cultures, we use the CE/BCE terms.

The abbreviation "O.S." ("Old Style") on some dates refers to the fact that the Russian Empire did not switch from the Julian to the Gregorian calendar at the same time as the rest of Europe, and therefore some figures and events have two dates.

Also, in the Julian calendar in England in the 16th century, the year began on March 25 rather than January 1. To avoid confusion with Gregorian dates, dates between January and March were often written using both years.

People and events whose original names are not in the Western alphabet have their native names (where possible) in the appropriate script shown in parenthesis. If you are using an e-reader to access an electronic version of this book, all characters don't always display on all devices.

A 50-year brass perpetual calendar.

Quote of the Day

"Time is an illusion, lunchtime doubly so."

Douglas Adams,
from *The Hitchhiker's Guide to the Galaxy*

Notes
and
Credits
Timespinner
Press

Cartoon by John T. McCutcheon

Copyright, Credit, and Contact

Follow Us

Our blog "This Day in History" (http://
timespinnerpress.com/this-day-in-history/) features short
articles on events and people associated with each day, and
updates several times each week. Also subscribe to the
"Quote of the Day" at http://timespinnerpress.com/quote-
of-the-day/. You can get daily links by following us on
Facebook at TimespinnerPress, or on Twitter as
@sidewisethinker.

Contact Us

Find an error or a format problem? Want information about
the series, about us, or about when the volume for your
special day might be available? Please email us at
editor@timespinnerpress.com. (We also take requests if your
special day isn't yet complete. Please give us at least six
weeks' notice if possible.)

Sources

We owe a great debt to Wikipedia, which is our first stop for
research. We attempt to make independent confirmation of
all important dates and facts through a variety of other
sources.

Other sources we frequently use include the Library of
Congress; "on this day" listings from *Encyclopedia Britannica*,
the *New York Times*, and the BBC; Omniglot for the names of
months in other languages; *Chase's Calendar of Events*; and, of
course, the always essential Google.

All art and photographs are either in the public domain, used under a Creative Commons license, or with a "fair use" justification, and most frequently come from Wikimedia Commons and the Library of Congress Prints and Photographs Division.

Attribution is provided where possible, or as requested by the copyright owner, or when there is particular historical significance, listed below. For information about any particular illustration or photograph, please contact us.

Credits

1. The cover photograph of Mohandas K. Gandhi was taken in the late 1930s, and is in the public domain in India, its country of origin, because it is an anonymous work published prior to January 1, 1957 (Indian Copyright Act of 1957, Chapter V, Section 25).

2. The illustration of the month of October used on the back cover is from the French Gothic illuminated manuscript *Les Très Riches Heures du duc de Berry* by the Limbourg Brothers, Jean Colombe, and an intermediate painter whose name is lost to history. It is in the public domain because its copyright has expired.

3. The box graphic used on the first page is from a 1916 pamphlet entitled "Divorce versus Democracy" authored by G. K. Chesterton, originally published in London by the Society of St. Peter and St. Paul. It is in the public domain in the US because it was published prior to 1923, and is in the public domain in all countries (including the country of origin) in which the copyright time is the author's life plus 70 years or less.

4. The graphic design for the section pages in this book is from a design originally created for a pharmacy label. It is courtesy of Wellcome Images (ICV No 11073, photo V0010813), and is used here under CC BY-SA 4.0.

5. The 1919 portrait photograph of US President Woodrow Wilson is from the Harris & Ewing Collection at the Library

of Congress (digital ID cph.3f06247). According to the Library, there are no known copyright restrictions on the use of this work.

6. The 1917 portrait photograph of John Logie Baird is from the collection of the Library of Congress Prints and Photographs Division (digital ID ggbain.25629). It is in the public domain because it was first published prior to January 1, 1923.

7. The photograph of John Logie Baird is from the November 1926 issue of *Popular Radio* magazine (Vol. 10, No. 7, pg. 650). It is in the public domain because although there was an original copyright, it was not renewed.

8. The image of the Opus Dei cross is used here under the terms of the GNU Free Documentation License, Version 1.2 or later.

9. The first *Peanuts* comic strip is copyright © 2005 by United Features Syndicate, and is used here under "fair use" provisions of US copyright law. No free alternative can exist because the characters are copyrighted and trademarked. It is a low-resolution image not suitable for the creation of counterfeit merchandise or the creation of illegal copies, it does not limit the copyright owner's rights to sell the comic strip in any way, and it is a significant image of a world-famous character presented here as part of a historical description of an important event.

10. *The Twilight Zone* logo, taken from a screen shot of the opening titles from the series, is used here under "fair use" provisions of US trademark law. It is ineligible for copyright as it does not meet the threshold of originality, but it is trademarked. Its use here is to illutrate an important show in the history of television for informational purposes, no free use version exists, and it is a low-resolution image not suitable for the creation of counterfeit goods.

11. The painting "October," from *Labors of the Month* by Simon Bening, was originally published in the first half of the 16th century, and is in the public domain because its copyright has expired.

12. The close-up photograph of Mohandas K. Gandhi was taken before 1942, and is in the public domain in India, its country of origin, because it is an anonymous work published prior

to January 1, 1957 (Indian Copyright Act of 1957, Chapter V, Section 25).

13. The 1940s publicity photograph of Groucho Marx is in the public domain because it was first published in the US between 1923 and 1977 without a copyright notice. Traditionally, publicity photographs are not copyrighted because of the way they are intended to be used.

14. The March 4, 1934, installment of *Flash Gordon* is copyright © 1934 and 1900 by King Features Syndicate, and is used here under "fair use" provisions of US copyright law. No free alternative can exist because the characters are copyrighted and trademarked. It is a low-resolution image not suitable for the creation of counterfeit merchandise or the creation of illegal copies, it does not limit the copyright owner's rights to sell the comic strip in any way, and it is a significant image of a world-famous character presented here as part of a historical description of an important event.

15. The 1902 photograph of Gandhi in South Africa is in the public domain because its copyright has expired, according to the South African Copyright Act No. 98 of 1978, amended 2002.

16. The 1520s portrait of Richard III is by an unknown artist. It is in the public domain because its copyright has expired.

17. The 2007 photograph of Sting at Madison Square Garden is by Lionel Urman, and is used here under CC BY-SA 3.0.

18. The 1950s publicity photograph of Abbott and Costello as hosts of *The Colgate Comedy Hour* is in the public domain because it was first published in the US between 1923 and 1977 without a copyright notice. Traditionally, publicity photographs are not copyrighted because of the way they are intended to be used.

19. The 1937 publicity photograph of George McFarland as "Spanky" in *Our Gang Follies of 1938* is in the public domain because it was first published in the US between 1923 and 1977 without a copyright notice. Traditionally, publicity photographs are not copyrighted because of the way they are intended to be used.

20. The wood engraving "The Discovery of Nat Turner" by William Henry Shelton was created between 1831 and 1876,

and is in the public domain because its copyright has expired.

21. The 1921 photograph of Ferdinand Foch by Melcy is in the public domain because its copyright has expired.

22. The 1912 painting "Nude Descending a Staircase No. 2" by Marcel Duchamp is in the public domain in the US because it was first published prior to January 1, 1923.

23. The 1830 self-portrait of Sarah Biffin is in the public domain because its copyright has expired.

24. The 1780 self-portrait of John André is in the public domain because its copyright has expired.

25. The woodcut of Fukuda Chiyo-ni by Utagawa Kuniyoshi is in the public domain because its copyright has expired.

26. The 1960 publicity photograph of Gene Autry is in the public domain because it was first published in the US between 1923 and 1977 without a copyright notice. Traditionally, publicity photographs are not copyrighted because of the way they are intended to be used.

27. The 1964 publicity photograph from *The Adventures of Ozzie and Harriet* is in the public domain because it was first published in the US between 1923 and 1977 without a copyright notice. Traditionally, publicity photographs are not copyrighted because of the way they are intended to be used.

28. The 1955 publicity photograph of Rock Hudson is in the public domain because it was first published in the US between 1923 and 1977 without a copyright notice. Traditionally, publicity photographs are not copyrighted because of the way they are intended to be used.

29. The 1945 trailer screenshot from *Rhapsody in Blue* is in the public domain because it was first published in the US between 1923 and 1977 without a copyright notice. Traditionally, film trailers are not copyrighted because of the way they are intended to be used.

30. The 1965 photograph of Alec Issigonis standing next to the first Mini and a 1965 model is courtesy of the Birmingham Museums Trust and used here under CC BY-SA 4.0.

31. The image "Fardier à vapeur" is in the public domain because its copyright has expired.

32. The 1879 painting of the Regent of Galuh is from the collection of the National Museum of World Cultures. The artist is unknown. The image is used here under CC BY-SA 3.0.

33. The photograph of popcorn from the 2015 PlayIT show in Budapest is by Christo, and is used here under CC BY-SA 4.0.

34. The 18th century painting Ángel de la Guarda is in the public domain because its copyright has expired. The artist is unknown.

35. The 1872 illustration by Alphonse de Neuville and Léon Benett from Around the World in Eighty Days is in the public domain because its copyright has expired.

36. The painting "October" is from the *Brevarium Grimani*, circa 1510, and is in the public domain because its copyright has expired.

37. The 1815 woodcut of a proposal is in the public domain because its copyright has expired.

38. The 1896 drawing "October" by Eugène Grasset is in the public domain because its copyright has expired.

39. The celestial sphere is from *Scenography of the Ptolemaic Cosmography*, by Johannes van Loon, based on Andreas Cellarius's *Harmonia Macrocosmica*, 1660. It is in the public domain because its copyright has expired.

40. The 1906 automobile calendar is by Edward Penfield, and is in the collection of the Library of Congress Prints and Photographs Division. It is in the public domain because its copyright has expired.

41. The 50-year perpetual calendar photograph is in the public domain.

42. The cartoon by John T. McCutcheon is from his 1905 collection *The Mysterious Stranger and Other Cartoons by John T. McCutcheon*. It is in the public domain because its copyright has expired.

License Description and Terms

Aside from material purely in the public domain, photographs and other material in this book are used under specific licenses permitting free use, usually with an attribution requirement. For full text and terms of these licenses, click or enter the appropriate links below. If you believe there is an error in the copyright status or attribution of any of these images, please email us.

- Creative Commons Attribution 2.0 Generic (CC-BY 2.0): http://creativecommons.org/licenses/by/2.0/deed.en
- Creative Commons Attribution-Share Alike 3.0 Generic (CC-BY-SA 3.0): http://creativecommons.org/licenses/by-sa/3.0/
- Creative Commons Attribution-Share Alike 2.5 Generic (CC-BY-SA 2.5): http://creativecommons.org/licenses/by-sa/2.5/deed.en
- Creative Commons Attribution-Share Alike 2.0 Generic (CC-BY-SA 2.0): http://creativecommons.org/licenses/by/2.0/deed.en
- Creative Commons Attribution-Share Alike 1.0 Generic (CC-BY-SA 1.0): http://creativecommons.org/licenses/by-sa/1.0/deed.en
- CC0 1.0 Universal (CC0 1.0) Public Domain Dedication (CC0 1.0) http://creativecommons.org/publicdomain/zero/1.0/deed.en
- GNU Free Documentation License (GFDL): http://en.wikipedia.org/wiki/Wikipedia:Text_of_the_GNU_Free_Documentation_License
- License Art Libre (Free Art License): http://artlibre.org

Other Books from Timespinner Press

The Story of a Special Day
Michael Dobson

A series of (eventually) 366 volumes covering everything that happened on your special day! Events, births, deaths, quotes, holidays, and much more. It's like a birthday card they'll never throw away!

US$7.95 print / US$2.99 ebook.

From Plassey to Pakistan
Humayun Mirza

The history of British Colonial India and the formation of Pakistan from the unique perspective of the son of Pakistan's first president and last of the royal line of Bengal, Bihar, and Orissa! This unique historical document tells the inside story of this distinguished family, including the detailed story of the coup that toppled his father from power!

US$27.95 print

A Whole New Navy: America's War in the Pacific

Miles Durr

The most comprehensive and detailed description of America's naval war in the Pacific ever—every battle, every ship, every task force and every task group from Pearl Harbor through the Japanese surrender! A must-have for the collection of every World War II buff!

US$29.95 print

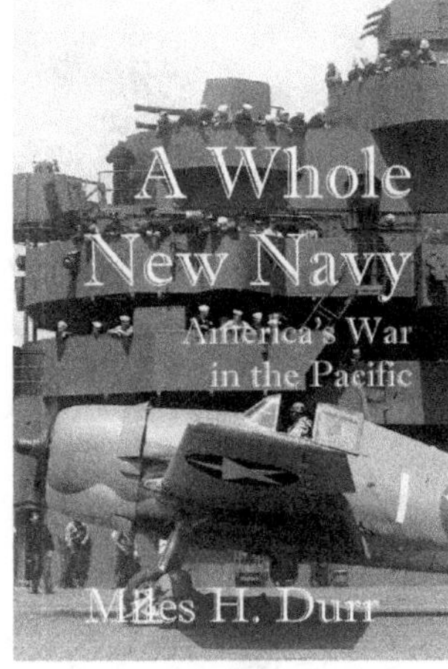

Improbable History: The Weird, the Obscure, and the Strangely Important

edited by Michael Dobson

From the birth of Western civilization to the rescue of Apollo 13, from the Leaning Tower of Pisa to Florence's Duomo, history has often turned on small, improbable details. Whatever happened to the ancient Samaritan people? Why did a fortuitous rainstorm allow the British to conquer India? How did an air raid in Italy lead to the development of chemotherapy? What happened when Albert Einstein met Adolf Hitler on the streets of Berlin? How did the Japanese manage to attack the US mainland using balloons? A cast of award-winning writers tackle some of the strangest tales in history!

US$19.95 print